Microsoft® Word
for the Macintosh
THE POCKET REFERENCE

Paul E. Hoffman

Osborne **McGraw-Hill**
Berkeley, California

Osborne **McGraw-Hill**
2600 Tenth Street
Berkeley, California 94710
U.S.A

For information on translations and book distributors outside
of the U.S.A., please write to Osborne **McGraw-Hill** at the
above address.

Microsoft® Word for the Macintosh™

1234567890 DODO 898

ISBN 0-07-881403-0

CONTENTS

This Pocket Reference is a complete and concise guide on how to use Microsoft Word for the Macintosh. It is useful for beginners who need to know about each command and for advanced users who want a quick reference. Information can be found in the Pocket Reference often more quickly than in Word manuals.

The commands and actions discussed in this reference cover Microsoft Word version 3.01. If you are using version 1.05, you should upgrade to version 3.01, which contains more features. Beginning and intermediate Word users wanting to learn more about Word's features should read *Microsoft Word Made Easy for the Macintosh* by Paul Hoffman (Berkeley, Calif.: Osborne/McGraw-Hill, 1987).

The following Macintosh keyboard conventions are used throughout this Pocket Reference.

- Command-key equivalents are shown in uppercase letters. The COMMAND key is often marked on keyboards with a cloverleaf symbol. When using COMMAND, OPTION, and SHIFT, you must hold them down while pressing the next characters of the command sequence. For example, to execute COM-

MAND, then press and hold SHIFT; while continuing to hold COMMAND and SHIFT, press >.

- Keys on the numeric keypad are prefaced with the word "KEYPAD." For example, KEYPAD-7 means press the 7 key on the numeric keypad. Note that not all Macintoshes have numeric keypads.

- A command name is followed by the name of the menu in which the command is located. For example, "the Section command in Format menu" describes the Section command.

- When an action requires clicking a button or giving a number in a dialog box, the dialog box is named the same as the command that led to it. Suppose, for example, you want to change the measurement units, you would use "the Measure buttons in the Preferences dialog box."

This pocket reference is divided into three sections: The first section contains general suggestions for using Word; the second section discusses Word's various menus and key combinations; the third section presents an alphabetical guide to Word's functions and features, their purpose, how to use them, and what results to expect.

GENERAL SUGGESTIONS

The following list contains useful tips to keep in mind when using the powerful features of Microsoft Word.

- Always work in full-menu mode. If the last command in the Edit menu is Full Menus, select that command. When exiting Word, the program remembers whether you were in short- or full-menu mode and will start in that mode next time.

- If you are aligning text in tables, use the Show Paragraph command in the Edit menu to display tab characters, spaces, paragraph symbols, and line-ending marks.

- When formatting text, it is easier to first type the text unformatted, select the text and then add formatting. Since some character formats are difficult to read, such as italic and small font sizes, typing them unformatted and later adding formats allows you to see what you have typed.

- Word's style sheets can be very helpful when formatting documents and reports. Use styles to make universal style changes easily and to give your work a professional appearance.

- If your keyboard has a numeric keypad and you want to use it to enter numbers, press the CLEAR key; the box in the lower left of the window will display "Num. Lock" to indicate that the keypad is locked in the number mode. Press CLEAR again to unlock the number mode.

- Often overlooked is Word's ability to customize menus. Frequently-used files can be added to the Work menu and formatting options can be added to the Format and Font menus. See CUSTOM MENUS for more information.

- Use Styles whenever possible. Styles allow you to globally change text formats. For example, if you have based all styles on Normal style and wish to change from a single- to a double-spaced document, simply change Normal style to double space. Your entire document automatically changes.

- Remember, formats can produce varied results with different printers. For example, columns in a table formatted for an Image-Writer may shift positions when printed on a LaserWriter. Character formats also vary. Underlining on the LaserWriter, for example, cuts off character descenders (such as g, p, q, y, and so on), while underlining on the ImageWriter does not.

- When printing on a LaserWriter from Word, use LaserWriter fonts such as Helvetica or Times. The results are more pleasing. Laser-Writer fonts also speed printing because fonts used by other printers are first translated by the LaserWriter.

- Do not use Macintosh special characters in your Word documents if you intend to export the documents to another computer. Most Macintosh non-alphanumeric characters differ from other computers. For example, a bullet (OPTION-8) does not appear as a bullet on an IBM PC.

USING THE KEYBOARD AND MOUSE

Moving the Insertion Point With the Keypad

Key	Action
← or KEYPAD-4	Moves insertion point one character to left
→ or KEYPAD-6	Moves insertion point one character to right
COMMAND-← or COMMAND-KEYPAD-4	Moves insertion point one word to left
COMMAND-→ or COMMAND-KEYPAD-6	Moves insertion point one word to right
↑ or KEYPAD-8	Moves insertion point up one line (insertion point remains vertically aligned with its previous position)
↓ or KEYPAD-2	Moves insertion point one line down (insertion point remains vertically aligned with its previous position)

COMMAND-↑ or COMMAND-KEYPAD-8	Moves insertion point up one paragraph
COMMAND-↓ or COMMAND-KEYPAD-2	Moves insertion point up one paragraph
KEYPAD-7	Moves insertion point to beginning of line
KEYPAD-1	Moves insertion point to end of line
COMMAND-KEYPAD-7	Moves insertion point to beginning of sen- tence
COMMAND-KEYPAD-1	Moves insertion point to end of sentence
COMMAND-KEYPAD-5	Moves insertion point to upper-left corner of screen
KEYPAD-9	Moves insertion point up one screen
KEYPAD-3	Moves insertion point down one screen
COMMAND-KEYPAD-9	Moves insertion point to beginning of docu- ment

COMMAND-KEYPAD-3	Moves insertion point to end of document
COMMAND-OPTION-[	Scrolls up one line without moving insertion point
COMMAND-OPTION-/	Scrolls down one line without moving insertion point
COMMAND-OPTION-Z or KEYPAD-0	Moves insertion point to its previous location (can be used for up to three previous locations)

Moving the Insertion Point Without the Keypad

(Note: OPTION-COMMAND-'-X means that you press OPTION-COMMAND-' and then press OPTION-COMMAND-X.)

Key	Action
OPTION-COMMAND-K	Moves insertion point one character to left
OPTION-COMMAND-L	Moves insertion point one character to right
OPTION-COMMAND-J	Moves insertion point one word to left
OPTION-COMMAND-SEMICOLON	Moves insertion point one word to right
OPTION-COMMAND-O	Moves insertion point up one line (insertion point remains vertically aligned with its previous position)
OPTION-COMMAND-COMMA	Moves insertion point down one line (insertion point remains vertically aligned with its previous position)

OPTION-COMMAND-Y	Moves insertion point up one paragraph
OPTION-COMMAND-B	Moves insertion point down one paragraph
OPTION-COMMAND-'-K	Moves insertion point to beginning of line
OPTION-COMMAND-'-L	Moves insertion point to end of line
OPTION-COMMAND-'-J	Moves insertion point to beginning of sentence
OPTION-COMMAND-'-SEMICOLON	Moves insertion point to end of sentence
OPTION-COMMAND-'-O	Moves insertion point to upper-left corner of screen
OPTION-COMMAND-'-COMMA	Moves insertion point to lower-right corner of screen
OPTION-COMMAND-P	Moves insertion point up one screen
OPTION-COMMAND-PERIOD	Moves insertion point down one screen

OPTION-COMMAND-'-P	Moves insertion point to beginning of document
OPTION-COMMAND-'-PERIOD	Moves insertion point to end of document

Selecting Text With the Mouse and Keypad

Key	Action
CLICK	Sets insertion point
DRAG	Extends selection
SHIFT-CLICK	Extends selection to current point (previous selection is extended or selection is made from previous insertion point)
DOUBLE-CLICK	Selects word
COMMAND-CLICK	Selects sentence
OPTION-DRAG	Extends selection in column
CLICK (selection bar)	Selects line

DOUBLE-CLICK (selection bar)	Selects paragraph
COMMAND-CLICK (selection bar)	Selects entire document
COMMAND-OPTION-M	Selects entire document
SHIFT-KEYPAD-4	Selects previous character
SHIFT-KEYPAD-6	Selects next character
SHIFT-COMMAND-KEYPAD-4	Selects previous word
SHIFT-COMMAND-KEYPAD-6	Selects next word
SHIFT-COMMAND-7	Selects previous sentence
SHIFT-COMMAND-1	Selects next sentence

Selecting Text Without the Keypad

(Note: OPTION-COMMAND-'-X means that you press OPTION-COMMAND-' and then press OPTION-COMMAND-X.)

Key	Action
SHIFT-OPTION-COMMAND-K	Selects previous character
SHIFT-OPTION-COMMAND-L	Selects next character
SHIFT-OPTION-COMMAND-J	Selects previous word
SHIFT-OPTION-COMMAND-SEMICOLON	Selects next word
SHIFT-OPTION-COMMAND-'-J	Selects previous sentence
SHIFT-OPTION-COMMAND-'-SEMICOLON	Selects next sentence

Inserting Special Characters

Key	Use
SPACEBAR	Inserts a normal space
OPTION-SPACEBAR	Inserts a nonbreaking space (cannot be broken at end of line)
TAB	Inserts a tab character
COMMAND-~	Inserts a nonbreaking hyphen (cannot be broken at end of line)
OPTION-HYPHEN	Inserts an optional hyphen
RETURN or ENTER	Inserts a paragraph mark
COMMAND-OPTION-RETURN	Inserts a paragraph mark after insertion point (allows you to continue typing in current paragraph)
SHIFT-RETURN	Inserts a new-line character (breaks to new line)
SHIFT-ENTER	Inserts a page break mark

COMMAND-ENTER	Inserts a section mark
COMMAND-OPTION-\	Begins formula (see FORMULAS)
COMMAND-OPTION-Q	Enters a character in ASCII code; finds ASCII code of a character
OPTION-\	<< character for form letters
SHIFT-OPTION-\	>> character for form letters

Deleting Text

Key	Action
BACKSPACE	Deletes character to left of insertion point or to left of selected character
COMMAND-OPTION-BACKSPACE	Deletes previous word
COMMAND-OPTION-F	Deletes character to right of insertion point or to right of selected character
COMMAND-OPTION-G	Deletes word to right of insertion point or to right of selected character

Using Windows

Key	Action
COMMAND-OPTION-W	Activates next window
COMMAND-OPTION-]	Zooms window to full-screen size or returns zoomed window to previous size
COMMAND-OPTION-S	Splits window
SHIFT-COMMAND-OPTION-S	Opens and closes footnote window

Menu Commands

Key	Command
COMMAND-B	Styles command in Format menu
COMMAND-C	Copy command in Edit menu
COMMAND-D	Character command in Format menu
COMMAND-E	Footnote command in Document menu
COMMAND-F	Find command in Search menu
COMMAND-G	Go To command in Search menu
COMMAND-H	Change command in Search menu
COMMAND-I	Insert Graphics command in Edit menu
COMMAND-J	Repaginate command in Document menu
COMMAND-K	Glossary command in Edit menu

COMMAND-L	Spelling command in Document menu
COMMAND-M	Paragraph command in Format menu
COMMAND-N	New command in File menu
COMMAND-O	Open command in File menu
COMMAND-P	Print command in File menu
COMMAND-Q	Quit command in File menu
COMMAND-R	Show Ruler command in Format menu
COMMAND-S	Save command in File menu
COMMAND-T	Define Styles command in Format menu
COMMAND-U	Outlining command in Document menu
COMMAND-V	Paste command in Edit menu
COMMAND-W	Close command in File menu

COMMAND-X	Cut command in Edit menu
COMMAND-Y	Show Paragraph command in Edit menu
COMMAND-Z	Undo command in Edit menu
COMMAND-=	Calculate command in Document menu

Character Formatting Commands

Key	Format
COMMAND-SHIFT-B	Bold
COMMAND-SHIFT-D	Outline
COMMAND-SHIFT-E	Change font
COMMAND-SHIFT-H	Small caps
COMMAND-SHIFT-I	Italic
COMMAND-SHIFT-K	All caps
COMMAND-SHIFT-Q	Symbol font
COMMAND-SHIFT-U	Underline
COMMAND-SHIFT-W	Shadow
COMMAND-SHIFT-X	Hidden

COMMAND-SHIFT-SPACEBAR	Plain text
COMMAND-SHIFT-PLUS	Superscript
COMMAND-SHIFT-MINUS	Subscript
COMMAND-SHIFT- <	Decrease font size
COMMAND-SHIFT- >	Increase font size
COMMAND-SHIFT-[	Double underline
COMMAND-SHIFT-]	Word underline
COMMAND-SHIFT-\	Dotted underline
COMMAND-SHIFT-/	Strikethrough

Paragraph Formatting Commands

Key	Format
COMMAND-SHIFT-C	Centered
COMMAND-SHIFT-F	First-line indent
COMMAND-SHIFT-G	Side-by-side
COMMAND-SHIFT-J	Justified
COMMAND-SHIFT-L	Flush left
COMMAND-SHIFT-M	Unnest
COMMAND-SHIFT-N	Nest
COMMAND-SHIFT-O	Space before 12 points
COMMAND-SHIFT-P	Plain paragraph
COMMAND-SHIFT-R	Flush right
COMMAND-SHIFT-S	Apply style
COMMAND-SHIFT-T	Hanging indent
COMMAND-SHIFT-Y	Double space

Additional Commands

Key	Format
COMMAND-OPTION-A	Repeat last find
COMMAND-OPTION-C	Copy to destination
COMMAND-OPTION-D	Change text to drawing in Clipboard
COMMAND-OPTION-R	Search for formatting
COMMAND-OPTION-V	Copy formatting to destination
COMMAND-OPTION-X	Move to destination

FUNCTIONS AND FEATURES

▶ Again

KEY:

COMMAND-A

EXPLANATION: Repeats previous editing command. Use the Again command to repeat typed text or to duplicate complex formatting commands. The last logical set of commands, from one insertion point movement to another, is executed on newly selected text. Note that this does not repeat a Find command; see FIND AGAIN for that action.

▶ Alignment

see PARAGRAPH ALIGNMENT

► All Caps

MENU AND KEY:

Character command in the Format menu

COMMAND-SHIFT-K

EXPLANATION: Changes characters to uppercase. However, Word does not actually convert characters, but only *displays* them in uppercase. For example, when a file is saved as text only, characters remain in mixed case.

► Bold

MENU AND KEY:

Character command in the Format menu

COMMAND-SHIFT-B

EXPLANATION: Changes selected characters to boldface.

▶ Borders and Boxes

MENU AND KEY:

Paragraph command in the Format menu

COMMAND-M

EXPLANATION: Puts a border next to a paragraph or a box around a paragraph. The Border area of the Paragraph dialog box lets you select the border type and border thickness. The border types are

- None
- Box
- Bar
- Above
- Below

    The border thicknesses are

- Single
- Thick
- Double
- Shadow

Boxes and borders always go from the left indent to the right indent. A box surrounds the paragraph; a border goes either above or below the paragraph. A bar goes on the left margin, regardless of the left indent; however, if you are using facing pages, the bar goes on the left margin of even-numbered pages and on the right margin of odd-numbered pages.

▶ Calculate

MENU AND KEY:

Calculate command in the Document menu

COMMAND-=

EXPLANATION: Performs mathematical calculations on selected numbers. You must specify the type of calculation you want to make, unless you are going to perform addition. When you execute the Calculate command, the results are shown in the window's display box and placed in the Clipboard. To select a column of numbers for calculations, press OPTION while you drag on the column.

▶ Centered Paragraphs

see PARAGRAPH ALIGNMENT

▶ Change

MENU AND KEY:

Change command in the Search menu

COMMAND-H

EXPLANATION: Replaces old text with new text. Specify the text to be changed and specify the replacement text. You can use ^c to indicate text that is to be replaced by the contents of the Clipboard. You can also instruct Word to search and replace whole words only, or to match upper- and lowercase characters. See FIND for more information on searching for special characters.

▶ Character Formatting

MENU AND KEYS:

Character command in the Format menu

COMMAND-D (All formats)
COMMAND-SHIFT-B (Bold)
COMMAND-SHIFT-D (Outline)
COMMAND-SHIFT-H (Small caps)
COMMAND-SHIFT-I (Italic)
COMMAND-SHIFT-K (Uppercase)
COMMAND-SHIFT-U (Underline)
COMMAND-SHIFT-W (Shadow)
COMMAND-SHIFT-X (Hidden)
COMMAND-SHIFT-/ (Strikethrough)
COMMAND-SHIFT-[(Double underline)
COMMAND-SHIFT-\ (Dotted underline)
COMMAND-SHIFT-] (Word underline)
COMMAND-SHIFT-SPACEBAR (Plain text)

EXPLANATION: Applies formatting to characters. You can select the following formats from the command dialog box:

- Style (such as bold or underline)

- Font (such as Geneva or New York)

- Font size (such as 9 point or 12 point)

- Position (superscript, subscript, or normal)

- Spacing (condensed, expanded, or normal)

See also ALL CAPS, BOLD, DOTTED UNDERLINE, DOUBLE UNDERLINE,

FONTS, HIDDEN TEXT, ITALIC, OUT-LINE, PLAIN TEXT, SHADOW, SMALL CAPS, STRIKETHROUGH, SUBSCRIPT, SUPERSCRIPT, UNDERLINE, and WORD UNDERLINE.

Styles, position, and spacing can be added to the Format menu by pressing COMMAND-OPTION-PLUS and giving the Character command. Fonts and sizes can be added to the Font menu by pressing COMMAND-OPTION-PLUS and giving the Character command. (See also CUSTOM MENUS.)

▶ Chooser

MENU:

Chooser in the Apple menu

EXPLANATION: Lets you choose a printer. If you have more than one printer driver available, the icon for each printer appears in the Chooser window. Select the printer and the printer port. If you are using a LaserWriter and the Macintosh System version 6.0 or later, you can also select background print spooling.

► Clipboard

MENUS AND KEYS:

Cut command in the Edit menu
Copy command in the Edit menu
Paste command in the Edit menu
Insert Graphics command in the Edit menu
Show Clipboard command in the Window menu

COMMAND-X (Cut)
COMMAND-C (Copy)
COMMAND-V (Paste)
COMMAND-I (Insert graphics)
COMMAND-OPTION-D (Convert text to drawing)

EXPLANATION: Reads from and writes to the Macintosh Clipboard. The Clipboard lets you store text or graphics when editing in Word. It also enables you to import and export text and graphics from other Macintosh programs.

While running Word, any text placed in the Clipboard is stored as formatted. When you quit Word, the formatting in the Clipboard is lost; however, graphics are preserved.

To convert text from a Word document to a drawing in the Clipboard, select the text and press COMMAND-OPTION-D. This is useful when you have formatted text in Word (such as a table) and want to keep the text's format in a drawing.

If you have a large amount of text in the Clipboard before quitting Word, you will be prompted whether to save the Clipboard.

▶ Columns

MENU:

Section command in the Format menu

EXPLANATION: Sets the number of columns for each page in the section, and the distance between the columns. If you have more than one section in your file and also want sections to begin on new columns, set the Section Start option in the dialog box. You can preview the results using the Page Preview command in the File menu.

You can also set columns within a table; see TABS.

▶ Copy

MENU AND KEY:

Copy command in the Edit menu

COMMAND-C

EXPLANATION: Copies selected text to the Clipboard.

▶ Copy Format

KEY:

COMMAND-OPTION-V

EXPLANATION: Copies the format from one selected text to another. Select the text from which you want to copy a format, and press COMMAND-OPTION-V (the window box will display "Format to"). Select the text you want to reformat and press RETURN.

You can also copy formats to text following an insertion point. If you press COMMAND-OPTION-V when no text is selected, the window box will display "Format from." Select the text from which you want to copy a format and press RETURN; new formats are applied at the insertion point.

To copy character formats, select the characters; to copy paragraph formats, select a paragraph by double-clicking on the selection bar.

▶ Copy to Destination

KEY:

COMMAND-OPTION-C

EXPLANATION: Copies text to another position without using the Clipboard. Select the text you want to copy and press COMMAND-OPTION-C (the window box displays "Copy to"). Click on the position where you want the text copied, then press RETURN.

You can also copy text from another location to the insertion point. If you press COMMAND-OPTION-C when no text is selected (the window box will display "Copy from"). Select the text you want to copy and press RETURN; the text is copied to the insertion point.

▶ Custom Menus

KEYS:

COMMAND-SHIFT-PLUS (Add menu choices)
COMMAND-SHIFT-MINUS (Remove menu choices)

EXPLANATION: Adds and removes menu items. Press COMMAND-SHIFT-PLUS to change the pointer to +. This enables you to select a variety of items to add to the menus. Pressing COMMAND-SHIFT-MINUS and selecting a custom menu choice causes that choice to disappear. You can add:

- Character formatting to the Format menu
- Paragraph formatting to the Format menu
- Font names and font sizes to the Font menu
- Documents to the Work menu
- Glossary entries to the Work menu
- Style names to the Work menu

The Work menu displays the first time an entry is added to it. To add a file to the Work menu, press COMMAND-SHIFT-PLUS, give the Open command in the File menu and select a file. Word remembers the path to that file. To add a glossary entry, press COM-MAND-SHIFT-PLUS and give the Glossary command in the Edit menu. To add any of the formatting commands, give the Character, Paragraph, Section, or Styles command, and select the item you want on the menu.

▶ Cut

MENU AND KEY:

Cut command in the Edit menu

COMMAND-X

EXPLANATION: Removes selected text and puts it in the Clipboard.

▶ Define Styles

MENU AND KEY:

Define Styles command in the Format menu

COMMAND-T

EXPLANATION: Sets paragraph formatting styles. Use this command to create new paragraph styles and to change the name and formatting of existing styles. In the command dialog box, you can specify

- Style name
- Style formatting
- Style upon which current style is based
- Style of paragraph when typing in a style

To delete a style, select it from the list box and press COMMAND-X. To change a style name, select the file and edit the name. If you enter a name of a style that already exists, Word asks if you want to merge the selected style with the style that you are naming.

▶ Delete

MENU AND KEY:

Delete command in the File menu

EXPLANATION: Deletes files from the disk. Word shows you a standard-file dialog box from which you select the file to be deleted.

▶ Document Menu

MENU:

Document menu

EXPLANATION: Changes information in the entire document. The commands in this menu are

- Open Header
- Open Footer
- Footnote
- Repaginate
- Outlining
- Spelling
- Hyphenate
- Index
- Table of Contents
- Calculate
- Renumber
- Sort

▶ Dotted Underline

MENU AND KEY:

Character command in the Format menu

COMMAND-SHIFT-\

EXPLANATION: Places a dotted underline beneath selected characters. Do not confuse the dotted underline of this command with the dotted underline you see beneath characters in the hidden style.

▶ Double Underline

MENU AND KEY:

Character command in the Format menu

COMMAND-SHIFT-[

EXPLANATION: Places a double underline beneath selected characters.

▶ Edit Menu

MENU:

Edit menu

EXPLANATION: Manipulates Clipboard and glossary; also sets preferences. The commands in this menu are

- Undo
- Cut
- Copy
- Paste
- Insert Graphics
- Glossary
- Show/Hide
- Paragraph
- Short/Long Menus
- Preferences

► File Menu

MENU:

File menu

EXPLANATION: Specifies the file on which you want to work; also prints the file. The commands in this menu are

- New
- Open
- Close
- Save
- Save As
- Delete
- Page Preview
- Print Merge
- Page Setup
- Print
- Quit

▶ Find

MENU AND KEY:

Find command in the Edit menu

COMMAND-F

EXPLANATION: Searches for specified characters. If Word does not find the text for which you are searching before the end of the file, it asks you whether you want to begin the search from the beginning of the file. Word will find text in your document even if the characters for which you are searching are in a different case than the case you specified. If, for example, you want to search only for uppercase, use the Find dialog box to change search parameters. You can also instruct Word to search for whole words only.

You can use special characters in your Find command to make the search more general. The characters you can use are

To Find	Use
Any white space	^w
Tab mark	^t
Paragraph mark	^p
Newline character	^n
Section mark	^d

Optional hyphen	^-
Any character	?
A question mark	^?
A caret	^^

▶ Find Again

KEY:

COMMAND-OPTION-A

EXPLANATION: Repeats previous Find or Find Formats command. This command can be used repeatedly to search for the same text for formatting. The search can even be repeated after changing text or adding formats.

▶ Find Formats

KEY:

COMMAND-OPTION-R

EXPLANATION: Searches for text in a specified format. To find a particular character format, select characters that use the specified format. To find a particular paragraph format, select paragraphs that use the specified format.

▶ Flush-Left or Flush-Right Paragraphs

see PARAGRAPH ALIGNMENT

▶ Fonts

MENUS AND KEYS:

Font menu

COMMAND-SHIFT-E (Change font)
COMMAND-SHIFT-> (Increase font size)
COMMAND-SHIFT-< (Decrease font size)
COMMAND-SHIFT-Q (Use Symbol font)

EXPLANATION: Allows you to change fonts and sizes. The fonts and sizes in the Font menu can be selected directly. .

To change the font from the keyboard, press COMMAND-SHIFT-E (the window box displays "Font"). Type the font name and press RETURN. You need only to type as much of the font name needed to make the name unique. If you change to the Symbol font, simply press COMMAND-SHIFT-Q.

To increase font size from the keyboard, press COMMAND-SHIFT->; to decrease font size from the keyboard, press COMMAND-SHIFT-<. (Font sizes available from the keyboard are 7, 9, 10, 12, 14, 18, 24, 36, 48, 60, and 72.)

▶ Footers

see HEADERS AND FOOTERS

▶ Footnotes

MENU AND KEY:

Footnote in the Document menu

COMMAND-E

EXPLANATION: Places a footnote reference mark at the insertion point and opens footnote window for footnote text. You can choose automatically-numbered footnotes or specify a footnote reference mark (such as an asterisk) in the dialog box.

To open the footnote window without adding a new footnote, press the SHIFT key while dragging the split window bar at the top of the scroll bar, or press COMMAND-

OPTION-SHIFT-S. When the footnote window is open, scrolling through your document causes the footnote window to scroll as well.

To remove footnotes from your document, delete the footnote marks; the footnote text is automatically deleted. If you use automatically-numbered footnotes, the footnotes following the deleted ones are renumbered.

To change the format of footnote reference marks or footnote text, use the Define Styles command in the Format menu and change the *footnote reference* and *footnote text* styles. If you link your documents, you can control footnote numbering in the Page Setup command in the File menu by setting the starting footnote number for the document. Use **0** to start numbering at the next higher number than the last footnote in the previous file. You can use the same dialog box to also specify where footnotes are to appear (at the bottom of a page, beneath text, or at the end of a section).

▶ Form Letters

see PRINT MERGE

▶ Format Copy

see COPY FORMAT

▶ Format Menu

MENU:

Format menu

EXPLANATION: Sets formatting for document. The commands in this menu are

- Show/Hide Ruler
- Character
- Paragraph
- Section
- Styles
- Define Styles
- Plain Text
- Bold
- Underline
- Outline
- Shadow

Other formats can be added to this menu (see also CUSTOM MENUS).

▶ Formatting Characters

see CHARACTER FORMATTING

▶ Formatting Paragraphs

see PARAGRAPH FORMATTING

▶ Formatting Sections

see SECTION FORMATTING

▶ Formulas

KEY:

COMMAND-OPTION-\

EXPLANATION: Prints mathematical formulas based on special formatting commands. Formulas allow you to align characters on top of and beneath others and to use radicals, fractions, integrals, arrays, brackets, and borders. Formulas can be only one line in length.

Formula commands can have options that determine the format of a formula. Formula commands and options are preceded by

COMMAND-OPTION-\. Formula commands
have one letter and formula options usually
have two. The text on which formula commands operate is enclosed in parentheses.

To enter formula commands, use the Show
Paragraph command in the Edit menu or
press COMMAND-Y. The letters you type are
displayed as they are being entered. If you
want to see how a formula will look when it
is printed, use the Hide Paragraph command
or press COMMAND-Y again.

The formula commands and their options
are:

Action	Command and Options
Two-dimensional array	A The argument for this command is a list of items for the array. The options are AL (align left), AR (align right), AC (align center), CO*number* (number of columns), HS*number* (spacing between columns in points), and VS*number* (spacing between lines in points). For example, \A\CO2\HS36(42,55,x,y) creates a 2″ × 2″ array

with 1/2" between columns.

Full-height brackets

B The argument for this command is the item that you want in brackets. The options are LC*char* (left bracket), RC*char* (right bracket), and BC*char* (both brackets). The characters you specify are used for the brackets. If you use BC with {, [, (, or <, the right bracket will be the matching },],), or >. For example, to put the two-dimensional array above in full-height square brackets, you would use \\B\\BC\\[(\\A\\CO2\\HS36(42, 55,x,y)).

Displacement

D This command has no arguments and must be followed by empty parentheses. The options are FO*number* (displace to the right), BA*number* (displace to the left), and LI (draw a line from the previous character to the next character). For example, to put a half inch between *X* and *Y,* use **X\D\FO36()Y.**

Fractions

F The arguments for this command are the numerator and denominator of the fraction. For example, **\F(2Y+33X,27)** puts *2Y+33X* over *27.*

Calculus operators

I This command allows you to form an integral, summation (capital sigma), and multiplication (capital pi). The three arguments are the lower limit, upper limit, and the item. The options are SU (makes the operator a capital sigma), PR (makes the operator a capital pi), IN (makes the lower and upper limits displayed to the right of the operator), FC \ *char*

(fixed-height replacement character for the operator), and VC*char* (variable-height replacement for the operator). For example, to show an integral from 0 to 2n of $n(n+i)$, use
\I(n=0,2n,n(n+i)).

List of values   **L** This command makes a comma-separated list of values.

Overstrike   **O** This command allows you to overtype the arguments. The options are AL (align left), AR (align right), and AC (center align), with the default being center alignment. For example, to put a bar above an x, use
\O(x,\S\UP4(-)).

Radical (square root)   **R** With one argument, this command draws the argument inside a square-root sign, and with two arguments, this command draws the first argument it used as an exponent for the root of the second argument. For example, to draw the cube root of *45i+j*, use **\R(3,45i+j)**.

Super- and subscript

S The options for this command are UP*number* (move argument up a specified number of points) and DO*number* (move argument down a specified number of points). If no number is specified, Word uses 2 points. If you give two arguments, they are stacked with the first argument on top. For example, to indicate *n squared,* use **n\S\UP3(2)**.

Box

X The options for this command are TO (draw a top border), BO (draw a bottom border), LE (draw a left border), and RI (draw a right border). With no argument, Word draws a border around the argument. For example, to draw a line above *DTACK*, use \X\TO(DTACK).

▶ Full Menus

MENUS:

Full Menus in the Edit menu
Short Menus in the Edit menu

EXPLANATION: Lets you use all of Word's features. When using only short menus, you will not have access to the following:

- Delete command
- Formatting options for character, paragraph, and sections
- Glossaries
- Horizontal scrolling
- Hyphenation
- Index
- Insert Graphics command
- Math
- Numbering

- Options in many commands
- Outlining
- Preferences command
- Sorting
- Split windows
- Styles sheets
- Tab types
- Table of contents
- Work menu

▶ Glossaries

MENU AND KEY:

Glossary command in the Edit menu

COMMAND-K

EXPLANATION: Lets you type an abbreviation and tell Word to expand it to its full meaning. Each glossary entry has a glossary *name* and *definition*. *Name* is the abbreviation, and *definition* is the full meaning.

To create a glossary entry, type the glossary definition in your document and select it. Give the Glossary command in the Edit menu, type the desired glossary name in the dialog box, and click Define. If the glossary definition is in the Clipboard, type the desired glossary name and give the Paste command. To remove a glossary entry, select it in the scrolling list and give the Cut command.

To expand a glossary name to its definition, press COMMAND-BACKSPACE, type the name of the glossary entry (you will see the name you type in the lower-left corner of the window), and then press RETURN.

▶ Go To

see JUMPING TO A PAGE

▶ Graphics

KEYS:

Shift-drag
Drag

COMMAND-OPTION-D

EXPLANATION: Lets you stretch or crop (cut) graphics pasted in your document. Graphics can be imported from other Macintosh programs through the Clipboard.

Word treats graphics like characters. The following character formats will have a visible effect on graphics:

- Dotted Underline
- Double Underline
- Hidden
- Outline
- Shadow
- Strikethrough
- Subscript
- Superscript
- Underline
- Word Underline

Word places a border around the selected graphic so that you can see its boundaries. You can also use the border controls to stretch or crop the graphic.

To change the size of a graphic, press the SHIFT key and drag on one of the controls. The right control lets you shrink a graphic horizontally, the bottom control lets you shrink a graphic vertically, and the corner control lets you proportionally shrink graphics horizontally and vertically. To crop a graphic, or place it in a larger frame, drag the controls without pressing the SHIFT key. Double-clicking on a graphic returns it to its full size without cropping.

To convert text in your document to a graphic and place it in the Clipboard, select the text and press COMMAND-OPTION-D.

▶ Gutters

see MARGINS

▶ Headers and Footers

MENUS:

Open Header in the Document menu
Open Footer in the Document menu

EXPLANATION: Lets you put information at the top and bottom of each page in a document. Headers and footers must be set for each section in a document. Headers appear above the top margin and footers appear below the bottom margin (see also MAR-GINS).

If you select Facing Pages in the Page Setup dialog box, Word displays header and footer commands for even- and odd-numbered pages. Even-numbered pages appear on the left, and odd-numbered pages appear on the right. If you select First Page Special in the Section dialog box, Word displays header and footer commands for the first page.

Place text anywhere in a header or footer by first entering the text in the window and then clicking the page number, date, or time icon.

Position a header or footer vertically by giving the Section command in the Format menu. Enter the distance from the top or bottom of the page to where you want the header or footer to be positioned. You can also change the position in the Page Preview command. Remember to set the position for all sections in your document.

▶ Help

MENU AND KEY:

About Microsoft Word in the Apple menu

COMMAND-?

EXPLANATION: Provides help with Word. The Help command lets you choose a topic from a scrolling list. To get help, press COMMAND-

? (the pointer becomes a question mark) and select a topic from the menu.

▶ Hidden Text

MENU AND KEY:

Character command in the Format menu

COMMAND-SHIFT-X

EXPLANATION: Hides selected characters. Hidden text can only be seen by selecting Show Hidden Text in the Preferences command in the Edit menu. When hidden text is selected to be shown, it is displayed with a dotted underline. Use hidden text for making a table of contents or index (see TABLE OF CONTENTS and INDEX).

▶ Hide Paragraph

see SHOW PARAGRAPH

▶ Hide Ruler

see RULER

▶ Hyphenate

MENU:

Hyphenate command in the Document menu

EXPLANATION: Adds optional hyphens to selected text or to an entire document. The Hyphenate command prompts you with suggestions for the hyphenation of each word; Word can perform automatic hyphenation as well, without prompting you. Note that Word's rules for hypenation may not apply to all words; thus, automatic hyphenation sometimes inserts hyphens incorrectly.

▶ Hyphenation

KEYS:

HYPHEN (Normal)
COMMAND- ~ (Nonbreaking)
COMMAND-HYPHEN (Optional)

EXPLANATION: Causes a word to hyphenate. Normal hyphens are always displayed on the screen; Word splits a word at a normal hyphen when it appears at the end of a line. Nonbreaking hyphens are also displayed, but Word will not split nonbreaking hyphens, even when they appear at the end of a line.

Optional hyphens appear only when a word is at the end of a line and only when the hyphen is able to make the word break. The Hyphenate command in the Document menu adds optional hyphens to a document. Non-breaking and optional hyphens can be displayed by using the Show Paragraph command in the Edit menu.

▶ Indents

MENU AND KEYS:

Paragraph command in the Format menu
Ruler

COMMAND-M (Paragraph command)
COMMAND-SHIFT-F (First line indent)
COMMAND-SHIFT-L (Flush left)
COMMAND-SHIFT-M (Unnest)
COMMAND-SHIFT-N (Nest)
COMMAND-SHIFT-T (Hanging indent)

EXPLANATION: Moves paragraphs relative to the left and right margins. In the Paragraph dialog box, you can set a left indent, first-line indent, and a right indent. On the ruler, the top triangle on the left indicates a first-line indent, the lower triangle indicates a left indent, and the large triangle on the right indicates a right indent.

To make paragraphs with the first line indented, move the first-line indicator to the right of the left-indent indicator. To make paragraphs with hanging indents (that is, with the first line to the left of the rest of the paragraph), move the first-line indicator to the left of the left-indent indicator.

Use COMMAND-SHIFT-N and COMMAND-SHIFT-M to nest and unnest paragraphs. Press COMMAND-SHIFT-N to move the first-line and left-indent indicators to the right 0.5"; use COMMAND-SHIFT-M to move them to the left.

▶ Index

MENU:

Index command in the Document menu

EXPLANATION: Adds an index to a document. Mark index entries with **.i.** in hidden text and follow them with **;** in hidden text. For example, in the entry ".i.fan;", the ".i." and ";" are hidden text.

To add a second level to an index, separate the first level from the second level using a colon (:). For example, if you had a primary index heading of "rain" but wanted a sub-

sidiary entry of "box of", you would use
.i.rain:box of;.

You can add formatting to an index entry.
For example, to make text boldface or italic,
add **B** or **I** after the **i** in the mark, such as
.iB.diamond. To enter a range, add (after the
i in the first mark and) after the **i** in the
second mark. To include text instead of a
page number, follow the entry with # and the
text **.i.hounds#See pets;**, for example.

The Index command in the Document
menu creates a new section for an index or
replaces a current index.

▶ Insert Graphics

MENU AND KEY:

Insert Graphics command in the Edit menu

COMMAND-I

EXPLANATION: Pastes an empty graphic in a
document. The Insert command lets you paste
an empty graphic in a document and then
resize the graphic's frame to hold space in
your document.

▶ Italic

MENU AND KEY:

Character command in the Format menu

COMMAND-SHIFT-I

EXPLANATION: Puts selected characters in italic format.

▶ Jumping to a Page

MENU AND KEY:

Go To command in the Search menu

COMMAND-G

EXPLANATION: Goes directly to a specified page. Note that Word uses the same page numbers that were used the last time the document was printed or repaginated. If you have more than one section in your document, enter the page and section as P*number* S*number*. For example, to go to page 7 of section 5; enter **P7S5** in the dialog box.

▶ Justified Paragraphs

see PARAGRAPH ALIGNMENT

▶ Keeps

MENU AND KEY:

Paragraph command in the Format menu

COMMAND-M

EXPLANATION: Prevents Word from breaking a paragraph or group of paragraphs across a page boundary. In the Paragraph dialog box, specifying Keep With Next Paragraph ensures that a paragraph will be kept with the next paragraph (this is useful for headings). Specifying Keep Lines Together prevents Word from breaking a paragraph at the bottom of a page.

▶ Keyboard

see USING THE KEYS AND MOUSE

▶ Line Numbers

MENU:

Section command in the Format menu

EXPLANATION: Adds numbers to the beginning of each printed line. This feature is commonly used by lawyers and referred to as *pleading numbering*. When selecting line numbering, you can also choose whether to restart a count at the end of each page, at the end of each section, or consecutively throughout the document. You can also specify when to put line numbers in a document (such as every fifth line) and where to place numbers in relation to the left margin.

▶ **Line Spacing**

MENU AND KEYS:

Paragraph command in the Format menu
Ruler

COMMAND-M (Paragraph command)
COMMAND-SHIFT-Y (Double-space)

EXPLANATION: Specifies the amount of space between each line in a paragraph. Using the Paragraph dialog box, fill in the Line box with the height (specified in points) of each line. To tell Word to automatically determine height, enter **Auto**. For example, if you use 12-point characters and want double-spaced lines, enter **24 pt**. Spacing can also be selected from the ruler.

▶ Lines

see BORDERS AND BOXES and VERTICAL
TABS

▶ Linked Documents

MENU:

Page Setup command in the File menu

EXPLANATION: Combines files for printing.
In the Page Setup dialog box, you can specify
the name of a file to follow a current file in
the Next File box. All files in a list should be
in the same folder. When you print a file that
is in a list of files, Word prints the file, then
the next file, and so on.

You can specify a page number for the first
page in the Page Setup dialog in the Start
Page Numbers At box. Placing **0** in the box
causes Word to make the first page number
the page following the previous file. You can
also have Word continue the footnote and line
numbers in a similar manner.

The only operations that recognize file
links are: printing; repagination; generating a
table of contents; and generating an index.

Thus, you cannot have the Find command search a list of linked files.

▶ Margins

MENUS:

Page Setup command in the File menu
Page Preview command in the File menu

EXPLANATION: Specifies where text is to appear on the printed page. A margin is defined as the distance from the edge of a page to where text begins. To adjust margins, enter margin values in the Page Setup dialog box, or drag the controls in Page Preview mode. Note that laser printers cannot print the full page width and generally require a .5" margin.

If you select Facing Pages in the Page Setup dialog box, you can also specify a gutter. A *gutter* is the extra space that Word reserves on the inside margins (the right margin on even-numbered pages and left margin on odd-numbered pages). When printed, gutter space is added to the margin.

▶ **Math**

see CALCULATE

▶ **Menus**

see CUSTOM MENUS and FULL MENUS

▶ **Mouse**

see USING THE KEYS AND MOUSE

▶ **Mouseless Operation**

KEY:

KEYPAD-PERIOD

EXPLANATION: Lets you control Word menus without using a mouse. After pressing KEYPAD-PERIOD, you have five seconds in which to choose a menu. Menus are chosen one of three ways:

- Press the ← or → key.

- Press the first letter of the name of the menu. Word selects the left-most menu with that letter; thus, **F** selects the File menu.

- Type a number from **0** to **8**. A **0** is the Apple menu, **1** is the File menu, and so on; **8** is the Work menu, if it is present.

When the menu is pulled down, select a command from the menu by pressing the ↑ or ↓ key, or the first letter of the command you want, and then press RETURN to execute the command.

You can move around in a dialog box using various keys. The ← and → keys move between groups in the dialog. In a list box, the ↑ and ↓ keys move the selection in the list. The TAB key moves to the next text box, while SHIFT-TAB moves to the previous text box. Select a button by moving to the button and pressing COMMAND-TAB (this causes a dotted underline to flash beneath the button), and then press COMMAND-SPACEBAR to click the button.

▶ Move to Destination

KEY:

COMMAND-OPTION-X

EXPLANATION: Moves text without using the Clipboard. Select the text you want moved and press COMMAND-OPTION-X (the window box displays "Move to"). Click on the position where you want to put the text and press RETURN.

Text can also be moved from another location to an insertion point. If you press COMMAND-OPTION-X when no text is selected, the window box displays "Move from"; select the text you want moved and press RETURN.

▶ New

MENU AND KEY:

New command in the File menu

COMMAND-N

EXPLANATION: Opens a document window for a new file. The window is titled "Untitled*number*" where *number* is a sequential number within a session. If you use the Save command for windows titled in this manner,

Word interprets the command as *Save As*; this enables you to name the file.

New Window

MENU:

New Window command in the Window menu

EXPLANATION: Opens another window in the document currently being viewed. The New Window command lets you see two parts of a document simultaneously. To identify the windows, :1 and :2 are appended to the window names. Editing can be done and viewed in either window.

Numbering Lines

see LINE NUMBERS

Numbering Pages

see PAGE NUMBERS

▶ Numbering Paragraphs

see RENUMBER

▶ Open

MENU AND KEY:

Open command in the File menu

COMMAND-O

EXPLANATION: Opens a document. The menu list includes all Word version 3 files as well as the following:

- MacWrite
- Microsoft Works
- RTF
- Text (ASCII)
- Word version 1

You can open any file, but Word will name them "Untitled"; thus, you must save them under different names.

To list all files on the disk (instead of only the document-type files as previously discussed), hold the SHIFT key and select Open from the File menu.

▶ Open Header and Open Footer

see HEADERS AND FOOTERS

▶ Outline

MENU AND KEY:

Character command in the Format menu

COMMAND-SHIFT-D

EXPLANATION: Puts selected characters in Outline style. If a graphic is selected, an outline is drawn around it.

▶ Outlining

MENU AND KEY:

Outlining command in the Document menu

COMMAND-U

EXPLANATION: Switches you into or out of Outline mode, so that text can be entered and modified in a structured format. Word displays an icon bar at the top of the window, which allows you to change the level of the selected text, move the text, add body text, or hide lower levels.

The following Keypad keys can be used in outline mode:

Key	Action
←	Promote
→	Demote
↑	Move heading up
↓	Move heading down
COMMAND- →	Change (demote) a heading to body text
KEYPAD-PLUS	Expand text
KEYPAD-MINUS	Collapse text
KEYPAD-ASTERISK	Display all levels

If you do not have a Keypad, the following keys can be used in outline mode:

Key	Action
COMMAND-OPTION-T K	Promote
COMMAND-OPTION-T L	Demote
COMMAND-OPTION-T O	Move heading up
COMMAND-OPTION-T COMMA	Move heading down

COMMAND-OPTION-T >	Change (demote) a heading to body text
COMMAND-OPTION-T PLUS	Expand text
COMMAND-OPTION-T MINUS	Collapse text
COMMAND-OPTION-T *number*	Display up to a specified level of heads
COMMAND-OPTION-T A	Display all levels

▶ Page Breaks

KEY:

SHIFT-ENTER

EXPLANATION: Forces a page break. Page breaks can also be forced by selecting Page Break Before in the Paragraph dialog box.

▶ Page Numbers

MENUS:

Page Setup command in the File menu
Section command in the Format menu
Open Header command in Document menu
Open Footer command in Document menu

EXPLANATION: Controls page numbering. Insert page numbers in headers and footers by clicking on the page icon in the header or footer window (see also HEADERS AND FOOTERS). Inserting numbers without using headers and footers is specified in the Section command in the Format menu in the From Top and From Right boxes. The Page Numbers command also lets you specify whether page numbers are to restart at 1 in the section and how the page number are to appear (such as Arabic, Roman, and so on).

Use the Page Setup command in the File menu to control the beginning page number of a file. This is useful when files are linked for printing. You can set the first page number at 1 (or higher); however, if 0 is specified, Word continues numbering from the previous file.

▶ Page Preview

MENU:

Page Preview command in the File menu

EXPLANATION: Lets you view a document exactly as it will be printed. When using page preview mode, Word displays an overview of the pages. You can use zoom to view different areas of the screen, add or move page numbers (if you are not using headers and footers), or change margins, header, and footer positions. If you want to view your margin changes, double click on either page.

▶ Page Setup

MENU:

Page Setup command in the File menu

EXPLANATION: Lets you set the following parameters for document pages:

- Paper type
- Paper orientation
- Paper width and height
- Top, bottom, left, and right margins

- Different setups for odd- and even-num-
  bered pages
- Gutter size
- Default tab stops
- Widow control
- Footnote position
- Initial numbers for footnotes, pages, and
  lines
- Linked file

▶ Paragraph Alignment

MENU AND KEYS:

Show Ruler command in the Format menu
Ruler

COMMAND-SHIFT-C (Centered)
COMMAND-SHIFT-J (Justified)
COMMAND-SHIFT-L (Flush left)
COMMAND-SHIFT-R (Flush right)

EXPLANATION: Aligns left and right sides of
a paragraph with the margins. Select one of
the four following alignments from the icons
near the middle of the ruler:

- Flush left (aligned with left margin only)
- Flush right (aligned with right margin only)
- Centered (not aligned with either margin)
- Justified (aligned with both margins)

▶ Paragraph Formatting

MENU AND KEYS:

Paragraph command in the Format menu
Ruler

COMMAND-M (All formats)
COMMAND-SHIFT-C (Centered)
COMMAND-SHIFT-F (First-line indent)
COMMAND-SHIFT-G (Side-by-side)
COMMAND-SHIFT-J (Justified)
COMMAND-SHIFT-L (Flush left)
COMMAND-SHIFT-M (Unnest)
COMMAND-SHIFT-N (Nest)
COMMAND-SHIFT-O (Space before 12 points)
COMMAND-SHIFT-P (Plain paragraph)
COMMAND-SHIFT-R (Flush right)
COMMAND-SHIFT-T (Hanging indent)
COMMAND-SHIFT-Y (Double-space)

EXPLANATION: Applies formatting to paragraphs. The Paragraph command displays a dialog box and a ruler. The following formats can be set from the command dialog box:

- Line spacing
- Space before and after paragraph
- Side-by-side
- Page break before
- Keep paragraph together, or keep with next paragraph
- Line numbering
- Borders
- Tab leaders

Using the Ruler, you can set the following:

- Left indent
- First-line indent
- Right indent
- Tab stops
- Vertical bars
- Alignment (flush left, flush right, centered, and justified)
- Line spacing (single-, one-and-a-half-, and double-spaced)
- Open spacing

See also BORDERS AND BOXES, INDENTS, KEEPS, LINE NUMBERS, LINE

SPACING, PAGE BREAKS, PARAGRAPH ALIGNMENT, RULER, SIDE-BY-SIDE, SPACING, TABS, and VERTICAL TABS.

The side-by-side, keeps, page-break-before, borders, alignment, and spacing selections can be added to the Format menu by pressing COMMAND-OPTION-PLUS and issuing a Paragraph command. (See also CUSTOM MENUS)

▶ Paste

MENU AND KEY:

Paste command in the Edit menu

COMMAND-V

EXPLANATION: Inserts text or graphics from the Clipboard into the document. To view the contents of the Clipboard before using the Paste command, issue a Show Clipboard command from the Window menu.

▶ Plain Text

KEY:

COMMAND-SHIFT-SPACEBAR

EXPLANATION: Removes character formatting from selected characters.

▶ PostScript Style

MENU:

Define Styles in the Format menu

EXPLANATION: Lets you use PostScript commands for PostScript printers in Word documents. This feature is especially useful for headers and footers and for adding crop marks, lines, and pictures.

▶ Preferences

MENU:

Preferences in the Edit menu

EXPLANATION: Lets you set the following preferences:

- Measurement units in document (inches, centimeters, or points)
- Display text as it will appear on a printed page
- Show hidden text
- Keep a document and program file in memory

▶ Print

MENU AND KEY:

Print in the File menu

COMMAND-P

EXPLANATION: Prints your document. You can select the following options before printing a file:

- Range (print the whole document, just the selection, or a range of pages)
- Number of copies
- Automatic or manual paper feed
- Hidden text or no hidden text

Depending on the printer, the Print dialog box can contain other choices. You can specify another printer with the Chooser command in the Apple menu.

The following additional options are available for the Apple ImageWriter:

- Tall (adjusted printing for tall pages with graphics)
- Quality (best, faster, and draft)

The following additional options are available for the Apple LaserWriter:

- Print back to front
- Print a cover page
- Fractional widths (to reduce space between boldface words)
- Smoothing (for non-PostScript fonts and graphics)
- Font substitution (for non-PostScript fonts)
- Reduction or enlargement of each page

▶ Print Merge

MENU:

Print Merge command in the File menu

EXPLANATION: Lets you create form letters. A form letter consists of the *main document* and the *data document*. The main document consists of text to be included in each form letter and the *variable fields* (enclosed in chevrons << and >>). The chevrons are entered with the OPTION-\ and SHIFT-OP-TION-\ keys. Merge commands are also enclosed in chevrons. The data document consists of a line of variable-field names and many lines of data.

To print form letters, be sure that the main document and data document are in the same folder. The main document must begin with a DATA merge command followed by the name of the data document. With the main document as the active window, give the Print Merge command in the File menu.

The merge commands are:

Command	Meaning
ASK	Word prompts you to fill in a field when each letter is printed
DATA	Identifies data file

IF ... ENDIF	Inserts text if a field in the data file has a particular value. You can use the =, >, <, <=, and >= operators for numeric fields or the = operator for string fields. The command can also include ELSE: IF ... ELSE ... ENDIF.
INCLUDE	Inserts another Word file in main document
NEXT	Word reads the next record in a data file
SET	Sets contents of a field or prompts you once for the value before printing

▶ Printers

see CHOOSER

► Quit

MENU AND KEY:

Quit in the File menu

COMMAND-Q

EXPLANATION: Exits Word. If you have made changes to a file, glossary, or dictionary, or there is information stored in the Clipboard, Word will prompt you to save these before you exit.

► Redo Command

see UNDO

► Renumber

MENU:

Renumber in the Document menu

EXPLANATION: Numbers or updates numbers at the beginning of selected paragraphs. Many levels of numbering are possible. Select the paragraphs you want numbered, and execute the command. Your choices in the Renumber dialog are:

- Renumber all selected paragraphs, or renumber only paragraphs that are already numbered
- Starting number
- Number format
- Level style (individual number on each line, or cascading numbers)
- Remove current numbers

  The format for the numbers can be

To get this format:	Use:
Arabic (1, 2, 3)	1
Uppercase Roman (I, II, III)	I
Uppercase letters (A, B, C)	A
Lowercase Roman (i, ii, iii)	i
Lowercase letters (a, b, c)	a

If you use cascading numbers for subparagraphs (such as 1, 1.1, 1.1.1, and so on), you can use a period, hyphen, slash, semicolon, or colon between the numbers in your specification. You can also enclose the numbers in parentheses, square brackets, or curly braces.

▶ Repaginate

MENU AND KEY:

Repaginate in the Document menu

CONTROL-J

EXPLANATION: Recalculates page breaks and page numbers for a document. This is useful once you have changed text or margins. Do not display hidden text when repaginating. Note that it takes longer to save a repaginated file than an unrepaginated file.

▶ Repeating Editing Commands

see AGAIN

▶ Replacing Text

see CHANGE

▶ **Ruler**

MENUS AND KEY:

Show Ruler in the Format menu
Hide Ruler in the Format menu

COMMAND-R

EXPLANATION: Lets you view and change paragraph formatting. With the ruler, you can set the following:

- Left indent
- First-line indent
- Right indent
- Tab stops
- Vertical bars
- Alignment (flush left, flush right, centered, and justified)
- Line spacing (single-, one-and-a-half-, and double-spaced)
- Open spacing

▶ Save and Save As

MENUS AND KEY:

Save command in the File menu
Save As command in the File menu

COMMAND-S (Save command)

EXPLANATION: Saves a document on disk. If a document is already named, the Save command keeps the same name. If a document is unnamed or you choose the Save As command, Word prompts you to name the file you are saving. If you use the Fast Save option to save only changes, more space is used than normal, but the save operation is faster.

You have many formats to choose from when you save a file:

- **Normal** – Word 3.0's regular storage format.

- **Text Only** – Carriage returns are placed only at the end of paragraphs and all formatting is lost.

- **Text Only With Line Breaks** – Carriage returns are placed at the end of each line as it is displayed on the screen and all formatting is lost.

- **Microsoft Word 1.0 (also Microsoft Works)** – Word 1.0's regular storage format. Style sheets and other features new to version 3.0 are lost.

- **Microsoft Word (MS-DOS)** – Word for MS-DOS format. Style sheets and other features not available in Word for MS-DOS are lost.

- **MacWrite** – MacWrite 4.5 format.

- **Interchange (RTF)** – Microsoft's format for storing formatted text-only files. Few programs use this format.

Many Macintosh programs can read Microsoft Word files directly, although others require a text-only file. If you are saving text-only files, check whether the receiving application needs carriage returns at the end of paragraphs or at the end of each line.

▶ Search Menu

MENU:

Search menu

EXPLANATION: Searches for or changes data. The menu commands are

- Find
- Change
- Go To

▶ Section Formatting

MENU:

Section command in the Format menu

EXPLANATION: Applies formatting to sections. Section marks are added by pressing COMMAND-ENTER. Formats which you can set from this command's dialog box are:

- The section starting point (on the same page as the previous section, on a new column, on a new page, on the next even- or odd-numbered page)
- Placement of headers and footers relative to the page edge
- Page numbering (choose to show numbers on page or in headers and footers only; choose to restart numbering at 1 for the section; choose the style of numbers)
- Footnote placement within the section
- Line numbering (for legal documents)

- Number of columns to use and the distance between each of them

See also COLUMNS, FOOTNOTES, HEADERS AND FOOTERS, LINE NUMBERS and PAGE NUMBERS.

To create a new section, press COMMAND-ENTER. When you print your document, Word uses the Section Start setting to determine how to break the page for the section after the mark.

▶ Shadow

MENU AND KEY:

Character command in the Format menu

COMMAND-SHIFT-W

EXPLANATION: Puts selected characters in shadow style. If a graphic is selected, a shadow is put at the lower-right corner of the its border.

▶ Short Menus

see FULL MENUS

▶ Show Clipboard

MENU:

Show Clipboard command in the Window menu

EXPLANATION: Opens a window to display contents of the Clipboard. Editing cannot be done in this window.

▶ Show Paragraph

MENU AND KEY:

Show Paragraph and Hide Paragraph in the Edit menu

COMMAND-Y

EXPLANATION: Displays symbols for Word's special marks (such as paragraphs and tabs). When using this command, you will see the following symbols:

- Footnote reference
- Formula character
- Graphics
- Newline
- Nonbreaking hyphen
- Nonbreaking space

- Normal hyphen
- Normal space
- Optional hyphen
- Paragraph
- Tab marks

When the symbols are displayed, the command becomes Hide Paragraph.

▶ Show Ruler

see RULER

▶ Side-By-Side

MENU AND KEY:

Paragraph command in the Format menu

COMMAND-M

EXPLANATION: Causes Word to place two or more paragraphs next to each other in the printed output. To accomplish this, format the left and right indents of the paragraph, select them both, execute the Paragraph command, and then select Side-by-Side. You can view the results using the Page Preview command in the File menu.

▶ Small Caps

MENU AND KEY:

Character command in the Format menu

COMMAND-SHIFT-H

EXPLANATION: Changes selected lowercase characters to small uppercase characters (small caps). Characters already in uppercase are unchanged by this command. Word does not convert these characters to uppercase; it only displays them on the screen as small uppercase. For example, when you save the file as text only, the characters will be in mixed case.

▶ Sort

MENU:

Sort command in the Document menu

EXPLANATION: Sorts selected paragraphs in ascending order. If the first character on a line is a number, Word will sort in numerical order; otherwise, Word sorts in alphabetical order. To sort in descending order, press the SHIFT key while selecting the Sort command.

▶ Spacing

MENU AND KEYS:

Paragraph command in the Format menu

COMMAND-SHIFT-O (for space before 12 points)
COMMAND-M

EXPLANATION: Puts extra space before and after paragraphs. Use the Paragraph command to specify the amount of space you want before or after a paragraph.

▶ Spelling

MENU AND KEY:

Spelling command in the Document menu

COMMAND-L

EXPLANATION: Checks the spelling of selected text or of a document. As each word is checked, Word notes any unrecognized spellings. You can correct misspelled words or add new words to the dictionary.

▶ Starting Word

EXPLANATION: Begins Word. You can start Word from the Macintosh Finder in the following ways:

- Double-clicking the Word icon
- Double-clicking the icon of the document you want to edit
- Double-clicking Word's Help icon

▶ Strikethrough

MENU AND KEY:

Character command in the Format menu

COMMAND-SHIFT-/

EXPLANATION: Puts selected characters in strikethrough style. If the selected text is a graphic, it draws a line through the graphic.

▶ Styles

MENU AND KEY:

Styles command in the Format menu

COMMAND-B

EXPLANATION: Lets you choose a style for paragraphs. You must use the Define Styles command in the Format menu to set up your styles. See also DEFINE STYLES.

▶ Subscript

MENU AND KEY:

Character command in the Format menu

COMMAND-SHIFT-MINUS

EXPLANATION: Moves selected characters down 2 points (or the amount you specify in the Character command dialog box). The font size of the selected character is also reduced by 2 points.

▶ Superscript

MENU AND KEY:

Character command in the Format menu

COMMAND-SHIFT-PLUS

EXPLANATION: Moves selected characters up 3 points (or the amount you specify in the Character command dialog box.) The font size of the selected character is also reduced by 2 points.

▶ Switcher

KEYS:

COMMAND-[(Slide left)
COMMAND-] (Slide right)
COMMAND-\ (Go to Switcher)
COMMAND-, (QuickSwitch)

EXPLANATION: Lets you access Apple's Switcher program. If you are switching between Word and either Excel or MacPaint, you can use the QuickSwitch option for updating information quickly.

▶ Table of Contents

MENU:

Table of Contents command in the Document menu

EXPLANATION: Adds a table of contents to your document. Table of contents entries are marked with .c*number*. (in hidden text) and followed by ; (in hidden text). If an entry ends with a paragraph mark, you do not need to follow it with a hidden ;, such as **.c2.Introducing the Product;**, for example, where the **.c2.** and ; are hidden text.

The top-most level of the document should be marked with **.c1.**, the next level with **.c2.**, and so on. You do not need to use entries if your document is an outline formatted with Word's outline feature (see also OUTLIN-ING).

The Table of Contents command in the Document menu creates a new section for the table of contents or replaces the current table of contents. You can choose to show page numbers and the levels that you want to include in the table of contents. Each entry has a style that corresponds to the level indicated in the mark. For example, all entries marked .c1. are in **toc 1** style.

▶ Tabs

MENUS AND KEY:

Paragraph command in the Format menu
Show Ruler command in the Format menu

RULER
TAB

EXPLANATION: Inserts tab marks in your document. Tabs let you align characters for tables. Tab stops are specified on the ruler and are adjusted in the Paragraph dialog box. The four types of tabs are:

- Left (align left side of column with tab)
- Right (align right side of column with tab)
- Center (align middle of column with tab)
- Decimal (align decimal point in number with tab)

In a table, you can select a column by pressing the OPTION key while you drag over the selection. Columns can be cut and pasted for rearranging your table.

▶ Underline

MENU AND KEY:

Character command in the Format menu

COMMAND-SHIFT-U

EXPLANATION: Underlines selected characters. On some printers, character descenders will be cut off.

▶ Undo

MENU AND KEY:

Undo command in the Edit menu

COMMAND-Z

EXPLANATION: Reverses the previous editing action. You can undo the following:

- Typing
- Clipboard commands
- Formatting commands
- Index and table of contents creation
- Renumbering
- Sorting
- After you execute Undo, you can execute the command again to redo the action that was just undone.

▶ Vertical Tabs

MENUS:

Paragraph command in the Format menu
Show Ruler command in the Format menu

RULER

EXPLANATION: Puts a vertical line at the specified position on every line of the paragraph. This acts like a tab stop, but instead of affecting how the Tab key works, it displays a line.

▶ Window Menu

MENU:

Window menu

EXPLANATION: Allows you to switch windows. The commands in this menu are

- Show Clipboard
- New Window

Window names are added to the end of the menu as you open windows.

▶ Word Underline

MENU AND KEY:

Character command in the Format menu

COMMAND-SHIFT-]

EXPLANATION: Underlines each character in the selected word. On some printers, descenders will be cut off.

▶ Work Menu

MENU:

Work menu

EXPLANATION: Adds customized options to the menu bar. You can add documents, glossary entries, and styles to the Work menu. See also CUSTOM MENUS.

ALPHABETICAL COMMAND LISTS

Alphabetical Command List by Action

Add menu (COMMAND-OPTION-+)

Add paragraph ahead (COMMAND-OPTION-RETURN)

Again (COMMAND-A)

All caps (COMMAND-SHIFT-K)

Bold (COMMAND-SHIFT-B)

Calculate (COMMAND-=)

Cancel (COMMAND-PERIOD)

Centered (COMMAND-SHIFT-C)

Change (COMMAND-H)

Character (COMMAND-D)

Clear Character (COMMAND-SHIFT-SPACEBAR)

Clear paragraph (COMMAND-SHIFT-P)

Close (COMMAND-W)

Copy (COMMAND-C)

Copy looks (COMMAND-OPTION-V)

Copy text as picture (COMMAND-OPTION-D)

Cut (COMMAND-X)

Decrease font size (COMMAND-SHIFT-←)

Define Styles (COMMAND-T)

Delete character right (COMMAND-OPTION-F)

Delete word left (COMMAND-OPTION-BACKSPACE)

Delete word right (COMMAND-OPTION-G)

Dotted underline (COMMAND-SHIFT-\)

Double space (COMMAND-SHIFT-V)

Double underline (COMMAND-SHIFT-[)

Dyadic copy (COMMAND-OPTION-C)

Dyadic move (COMMAND-OPTION-X)

Expand Glossary (COMMAND-BACKSPACE)

Find again (COMMAND-OPTION-A)

Find (COMMAND-F)

First line indent (COMMAND-SHIFT-F)

Font change (COMMAND-SHIFT-E)

Footnote (COMMAND-E)

Formula (COMMAND-O)

Formula (COMMAND-OPTION-\)

Glossary (COMMAND-K)

Goto (COMMAND-G)

Graphic character (COMMAND-OPTION-Q)

Hanging indent (COMMAND-SHIFT-T)

Help (COMMAND-?)

Increase font size (COMMAND-SHIFT→)

Insert Graphics (COMMAND-I)

Italic (COMMAND-SHIFT-I)

Justified (COMMAND-SHIFT-J)

Keyboard menus (OPTION-TAB)

Left aligned (COMMAND-SHIFT-L)

More (COMMAND-OPTION-')

Move character left (←)

Move character left (COMMAND-OPTION-K)

Move character right (NUMERIC-4)

Move character right (→)

Move character left (NUMERIC-6)

Move character right (COMMAND-OPTION-L)

Move line down (↓)

Move line down (COMMAND-OPTION-COMMA)

Move line down (NUMERIC-2)

Move line up (↑)

Move line up (COMMAND-OPTION-O)

Move line up (COMMAND-NUMERIC-8)

Move page down (NUMERIC-3)

Move page up (NUMERIC-9)

Move paragraph down (COMMAND-NUMERIC-8)

Move paragraph down (COMMAND-OPTION-B)

Move paragraph up (COMMAND-NUMERIC-2)

Move paragraph up (COMMAND-OPTION-Y)

Move screen down (COMMAND-OPTION-PERIOD)

Move screen up (COMMAND-OPTION-P)

Move to document beginning (COMMAND-NUMERIC-9)

Move to document end (COMMAND-NUMERIC-3)

Move to line begin (NUMERIC-7)

Move to line end (NUMERIC-1)

Move to sentence (COMMAND-NUMERIC-7)

Move to sentence end (COMMAND-NUMERIC-1)

Move word left (COMMAND-NUMERIC-4)

Move word left (COMMAND-OPTION-J)

Move word right (COMMAND-NUMERIC-6)

Move word right (COMMAND-OPTION-;)

Nest paragraph (COMMAND-SHIFT-N)

New (COMMAND-N)

New Division (COMMAND-ENTER)

New page (SHIFT-ENTER)

New paragraph (RETURN)

Newline (SHIFT-RETURN)

Next window (COMMAND-OPTION-W)

No action (COMMAND-NUMERIC-5)

No action (NUMERIC-5)

Nonbreaking hyphen (COMMAND-')

Nonbreaking space (OPTION-SPACEBAR)

Nonrequired hyphen (COMMAND-MINUS)

Open (COMMAND-O)

Open spacing (COMMAND-SHIFT-O)

Outline (COMMAND-SHIFT-D)

Outline prefix (COMMAND-OPTION-T)

Outlining (COMMAND-U)

Paragraph (COMMAND-M)

Paste (COMMAND-V)

Print (COMMAND-P)

Quit (COMMAND-Q)

Remove menu (COMMAND-OPTION-MINUS)

Repaginate (COMMAND-J)

Right aligned (COMMAND-SHIFT-R)

Save (COMMAND-S)

Scan looks (COMMAND-OPTION-R)

Scroll up (COMMAND-OPTION-[)

Select whole document (COMMAND-OPTION-M)

Shadow (COMMAND-SHIFT-W)

Show Paragraph (COMMAND-Y)

Show Ruler (COMMAND-R)

Side-by-Side (COMMAND-SHIFT-G)

Small caps (COMMAND-SHIFT-H)

Spell (COMMAND-L)

Split Window (COMMAND-OPTIONS-S)

Strikethrough (COMMAND-SHIFT-/)

Style name (COMMAND-SHIFT-S)

Styles (COMMAND-B)

Subscript (COMMAND-SHIFT-MINUS)

Superscript (COMMAND-SHIFT-+)

Symbol font (COMMAND-SHIFT-Q)

Underline (COMMAND-SHIFT-U)

Undo (COMMAND-Z)

Unnest paragraph (COMMAND-SHIFT-M)

Vanish (COMMAND-SHIFT-X)

Word underline (COMMAND-SHIFT-])

Zoom (COMMAND-OPTION-])

Alphabetical Command List by Key Name

COMMAND-A: Again

COMMAND-B: Styles

COMMAND-C: Copy

COMMAND-D: Character

COMMAND-E: Footnote

COMMAND-F: Find

COMMAND-G: Goto

COMMAND-H: Change

COMMAND-I: Insert Graphics

COMMAND-J: Repaginate

COMMAND-K: Glossary

COMMAND-L: Spell

COMMAND-M: Paragraph

COMMAND-N: New

COMMAND-O: Open

COMMAND-P: Print

COMMAND-Q: Quit

COMMAND-R: Show Ruler

COMMAND-S: Save

COMMAND-T: Define Styles

COMMAND-U: Outlining

COMMAND-V: Paste

COMMAND-W: Close

COMMAND-X: Cut

COMMAND-Y: Show Paragraph

COMMAND-Z: Undo

COMMAND-HYPHEN: Nonrequired hyphen

COMMAND-PERIOD: Cancel

COMMAND-0: Formula

COMMAND-=: Calculate

COMMAND-?: Help

COMMAND-': Nonbreaking hyphen

COMMAND-BACKSPACE: Expand Glossary

COMMAND-ENTER: New Division

COMMAND-SHIFT-B: Bold

COMMAND-SHIFT-C: Centered

COMMAND-SHIFT-D: Outline

COMMAND-SHIFT-E: Font change

COMMAND-SHIFT-F: First line indent

COMMAND-SHIFT-G: Side-by-Side

COMMAND-SHIFT-H: Small caps

COMMAND-SHIFT-I: Italic

COMMAND-SHIFT-J: Justified

COMMAND-SHIFT-K: All caps

COMMAND-SHIFT-L: Left aligned

COMMAND-SHIFT-M: Unnest paragraph

COMMAND-SHIFT-N: Nest paragraph

COMMAND-SHIFT-O: Open spacing

COMMAND-SHIFT-P: Clear paragraph

COMMAND-SHIFT-Q: Symbol font

COMMAND-SHIFT-R: Right aligned

COMMAND-SHIFT-S: Style name

COMMAND-SHIFT-T: Hanging indent

COMMAND-SHIFT-U: Underline

COMMAND-SHIFT-W: Shadow

COMMAND-SHIFT-X: Vanish

COMMAND-SHIFT-Y: Double space

COMMAND-SHIFT-+: Superscript

COMMAND-SHIFT-MINUS: Subscript

COMMAND-SHIFT-/: Strikethrough

COMMAND-SHIFT-←: Decrease font size

COMMAND-SHIFT-→: Increase font size

COMMAND-SHIFT-[: Double underline

COMMAND-SHIFT-\: Dotted underline

COMMAND-SHIFT-]: Word underline

COMMAND-SHIFT-SPACEBAR: Clear character

COMMAND-OPTION-A: Find again

COMMAND-OPTION-B: Move paragraph down

COMMAND-OPTION-C: Dyadic copy

COMMAND-OPTION-D: Copy text as picture

COMMAND-OPTION-F: Delete character right

COMMAND-OPTION-G: Delete word right

COMMAND-OPTION-J: Move word left

COMMAND-OPTION-K: Move character left

COMMAND-OPTION-L: Move character right

COMMAND-OPTION-M: Select whole document

COMMAND-OPTION-O: Move line up

COMMAND-OPTION-P: Move screen up

COMMAND-OPTION-Q: Graphic character

COMMAND-OPTION-R: Scan looks

COMMAND-OPTION-S: Split Window

COMMAND-OPTION-T: Outline prefix

COMMAND-OPTION-V: Copy looks

COMMAND-OPTION-W: Next window

COMMAND-OPTION-X: Dyadic move

COMMAND-OPTION-Y: Move paragraph up

COMMAND-OPTION-Z: Jump to last insert

COMMAND-OPTION-': More

COMMAND-OPTION-+: Add menu

COMMAND-OPTION-COMMA: Move line down

COMMAND-OPTION-MINUS: Remove menu

COMMAND-OPTION-PERIOD: Move screen down

COMMAND-OPTION-/: Scroll down

COMMAND-OPTION-;: Move word right

COMMAND-OPTION-[: Scroll up

COMMAND-OPTION-\: Formula

COMMAND-OPTION-]: Zoom

COMMAND-OPTION-BACKSPACE: Delete word left

COMMAND-OPTION-RETURN: Add paragraph ahead

NUMERIC-1: Move to end of line

NUMERIC-2: Move line down

NUMERIC-3: Move page down

NUMERIC-4: Move character left

NUMERIC-5: No action

NUMERIC-6: Move character right

NUMERIC-7: Move to beginning of line

NUMERIC-8: Move line up

NUMERIC-9: Move page up

COMMAND-NUMERIC-1: Move to end of sentence

COMMAND-NUMERIC-2: Move paragraph up

COMMAND-NUMERIC-3: Move to end of document

COMMAND-NUMERIC-4: Move word left

COMMAND-NUMERIC-5: No action

COMMAND-NUMERIC-6: Move word right

COMMAND-NUMERIC-7: Move to beginning of sentence

COMMAND-NUMERIC-8: Move paragraph down

COMMAND-NUMERIC-9: Move to beginning of document

OPTION-SPACEBAR: Nonbreaking space

OPTION-TAB: Keyboard menus

RETURN: New paragraph

SHIFT-ENTER: New page

SHIFT-RETURN: Newline

↓: Move line down

←: Move character left

→: Move character right

↑: Move line up